THE LIES OF THE DATING PHASE

BY

STEPHEN ADEGBOYE

Table of Contents

INTRODUCTION

This term called "DATING" can fill the best of us with excitement, dread, or mixture of both. The first use of the word is often attributed to American columnist George Ade, in the Chicago Record in 1896.

So having your eggs in a number of baskets isn't unheard of in our modern-day dating culture, but this wasn't always the case. Once upon a time, you didn't date to find someone you had an amazing connection with, you courted to find someone respectable who wouldn't pour your inheritance down the drain.

Nichi Hodgson, author of the curious History of dating, explains that up until 1870, "women couldn't keep property or money or goods they inherited upon marriage, "until a law was passed which ended this.

"Because they had to give everything to the person they are married to, it really mattered that the person they married… wasn't going to spend the family fortune. Also, historically, divorces could only be granted by the king, so unless you were very well connected, it was vital you wouldn't come to regret your marriage further down the line.

But then your reasons for regretting a marriage didn't at this point extend to falling out of love. Infact, falling in love wasn't a prerequisite for marriage at all. However Nichi explained that during the enlightenment that all began to change, and by the time "Queen Victoria married Prince Albert, who was a love match- that's when the public perception of marrying for love started to shift.

STICKING TO RULES:

Unfortunately for eligible young ladies and gentlemen at that time though, the rules around courting were still incredibly strict. You had to take a calling card to the home of the woman you wanted to court, you had to be invited to come, everyone, your families had to agree on the match- The list goes on. But love was still a factor: "though there was still an element of people deciding that it was a good economic and social fit… if you said you were madly in love with someone and they were roughly of the same social standing and they had a bit of money, then that was generally seen as okay. "Nichi explains.

And once you'd arranged a date of sorts, one thing was absolutely vital: a chaperone. Chaperones were usually a member of your family, such as your mother or aunt, who would accompany you on your date to ensure everything, was above board and you kept your gloves on. But the "chaperon system went to pot" with the coming world war One says Nichi.

One reason for this was women were starting to work to aid the war effort, which increased their freedom immensely. However, one major factor in the decline of chaperons was the fact that women were allowed to cycle and they could do so on their own.

Women then started travelling on trains by themselves, which became a place for them to meet people. They would also travel to the seaside when they had time, which led to the development of the holiday romance.

SPOILT FOR CHOICE:

From this point on, the dating pool just got larger and larger- while the amount of choice people have these days seem overwhelming, back in the mid -20th century it was a luxury.

Nichi explains: it wasn't really until the 60s that people from all walks of life were actually mixing with each other and London for example was a melting pot of people of different ethnic and social backgrounds.

Then came up a soap opera titled Emergency Ward 10 that ran from 1957 to 1967 on TV that showed one of the first intimate moments to be seen on British TV and something of a watershed moment.

As Nichi puts it: "these things were slowly breaking down the barriers around what people could mix and who could go out with whom".

Then with the invention of the worldwide web, our dating choices became almost unlimited.

Source: BBC Bite size

I dedicate this life manual to God Almighty; He gave me the deep mysteries on a personal account to be able to share them with the world around me...

I also dedicate this book to everyone searching for deep mysteries on the depths of dating and enrollment into school of personal finding...

ACKNOWLEDGEMENT

Big thanks to my fathers in the Lord, my mentors, colleagues in the family life practioners industry, destiny friends and family members for their guidance, counseling, love and prayers in my life.

Thanks to God's servant, our father, my amiable youth pastor in charge of the Mountain of fire and miracle ministries region 5 in the city of Port Harcourt, Pastor Ralu Chinedu and his lovely wife, Mrs. Esther Udechukwu and the entire youth church of region 5, port Harcourt, thank you for welcoming me into your midst from day one.

Big thanks to my editor, Andriana all the way from Florida Miami in the United States for a job well done. Thanks for coming my way; I appreciate you for everything immensely.

Thanks to my married and unmarried counselees who have always trusted me with their details and lives, and helped me with the much needed insights coupled with my own personal experience in compiling this book

God bless you all….

CHAPTER ONE: THE SCIENCE OF DATING AND COURTSHIP

Ignite dating that is a blog online provided 5 stages of dating on determining whether your relationship has the strength to flourish into a long term commitment. And they are;

- Attraction
- Reality
- Commitment
- Intimacy
- Engagement

The problem with this dispensation is that, many young people jump phases and suddenly become confused in the confines of marriage, if they even make it to the marriage phase.

There is a very disturbing trend now where people get attracted to people because of their complexion, height, intelligence, physique and just immediately think they are in love, not knowing that they are just exhibiting their natural characteristics to react to liking what they are seeing.

So if we are to go by these five stages of dating, a person could just get attracted to someone, and skip the reality and commitment phases and want intimacy with a total stranger already. Intimacy here may not even mean physical intimacy in terms of sleeping together, but a mind alignment that can erupt under the premise of falsehood and a lack of wisdom in managing your heart that is filled with emotions already.

Why the reality phase is very important is because, you are supposed to have come to terms with some physical traits, character flaws and weaknesses and still convince yourself into thinking that you are still definitely compactible with that particular person in spite of all that you have seen.

Commitment to what you have aligned your mind means you are signing a warrant that you will be held responsible for anything that happens to you and your mental/ emotional health system if it does end in marriage.

In my counseling experiences with counseling many married and unmarried people, have seen how faulty the attraction has been which unfortunately made many of them to believe a fake reality because of a poorly laid foundation which sometimes can be as a result of many unfulfilled relationships and marriages.

I have seen many people who have come to terms with potential realities in their "would be marriage unions" with the persons they were first attracted to and have found out that there are so many questionable variables but still went ahead for an engagement they allowed intimacy phase which is the fourth dimension to cloud their emotions and weaken their senses of judgments instead of focusing on why they were attracted and understanding if this attraction will always be there for a very long time.

Imagine a scenario where it was a woman's buttocks that got a man attracted to her. So after getting attracted, the reality phase is supposed to make him understand that those buttocks won't always be the way they are as time goes on especially as age catches up with her, so he is supposed to weigh his options before committing which is actually the third phase.

This is why a man will marry his wife, and still feel the need to delve into infidelity because he suddenly feels unsatisfied with what his wife has in store. I stand to be corrected, **one of the lies of the dating phase**

is to think that attraction is love, because if attraction is truly love, all potential meet ups in different places will always definitely end up in successful and blissful marriages.

Now, this is about to get interesting because we are looking at a system that is worldly renowned for bringing people together for various reasons and leaving many people sad and unfulfilled in the confines of marriage and many more with wounds being carried in their hearts just because of varying methodologies.

So, pediaa.com has this to say on what dating and courtship is all about with this tabular illustration:-

DATING	COURTSHIP
Casually getting to know someone, you may eventually have a romantic relationship with.	It is being romantically involved with someone with the intention of marrying him or her.
May or may not end up in marriage	Ends up in marriage
Doesn't involve parental approval and supervision.	Usually involves it
Could involve sexual intimacy	Does not involve sexual intimacy
Can be casual and not involve any deep emotions	Very serious and involves deep emotions.

The truth is this, the bible didn't expressly talk about dating in the bible but of course courtship was seen and experienced and even documented in some passages which we would elucidate on as we progress in this book, but because of what this dispensation has turned into and where we are at the moment, marrying it with how fast things have changed in the different centuries, it is very imperative to understand how scriptures can shed light on the current dating scene that takes many shape in so many part of the world.

In my counseling experiences with confused singles that are my counselees, they are usually frustrated with, in their view, the bible's lack of relevance and direction to the dating scene. So even while the bible doesn't give a step by step or "how to" instructions, we can look at several stories from scriptures that shed light on our current relationship scene and provide timeless principles that still apply today.

Principle one: - (Spiritual unity)

One of the biggest mistakes Christian singles make is to find themselves entangled with non-believers. Imagine being asked to send your nude pictures as a lady online to a guy you are just got attracted to online, who out of your desperation, you started dating. Many singles get so desperate in their search for "the One" that they compromise in this most crucial area of spiritual compatibility.

The bible clearly says believers shouldn't date or marry someone who is not a fellow Christ follower (2 Corinthians 6:14-15; 1 Corinthians 7:39). If you are in a dating relationship with someone who isn't a Christian, then you are outside of God's will for your life.

My father in the lord, Prof. Dk Olukoya, once said that being in a relationship with a God fearing person makes up for over 75% of the needed criteria in being with someone already. So don't even pray about whether it's right or not; don't waste your pastor's time asking him. God has spoken on this issue in His word; it's not a grey area. You must date and marry a believer if you want God to bless you relationship.

Principle two:- (Sexual purity)

We live in a sexually saturated society. It seems like everyone these days is either having sex or at least talking about every detail of their sex lives. Despite the increased openness to discussing sex, people are still not satisfied with the end result.

Years ago, Jesus met a woman who had persistently tried to find meaning from her relationships with men. Jesus told her He could give her living water that would quench her thirst forever. Her experience with Christ forever changed her outlook on life. After her conversation with Jesus, she went back into town and told everyone about the Lord's power. Her story led to a major spiritual awakening in her community.

That's fine and well and biblical, 'you say. "But as a single person would ask, what am I supposed to do with a raging sex drive?" I like what John Piper said in his book "future Grace", "The fire of lust's pleasures must be fought with the fire of God's pleasures. If we try to fight the fire of lust with prohibitions and threats alone, even with the terrible warnings of Jesus, we will fail. We must fight it with a massive promise of superior happiness.

Principle three:- (Rock Solid Character)

Relationship expert Dr Henry Cloud says' "in a relationship, we are attracted to what we see on the outside, it's always about the looks and personality; but in a long term relationship, what we end up experiencing is what's on the inside, their character.

A large part of succeeding in the dating game rests on your ability to discern whether or not the person you are going out with has a rock solid character. If the person is habitually late, never pays bills on time, or can't hold a job for more than six months, it is a sign of weak character. If you are going to be spending the rest of your life with someone, be sure he or she can follow through on commitments, take responsibility for actions and endure hard times with great faith.

Principle Four (Time)

Far too many couples are in way too big a hurry to get hitched. Granted, you don't need to date someone for 14 years before you get married. But you do need to take your precious time in the dating game if you want to win on the long run. It takes time to get to know what someone is really like. It takes time to see if someone has what it takes to be a mate for life. If you are rushing things, then you are playing Russian roulette with your love life already.

Getting entangled with the right person can be fun; going about missing it in the confines of dating can be painful too. But make no mistake about it; this subject matter is a serious business. Why? Because everything rides on whom you decide to date and marry. That's why you cannot afford to get in too big hurry to tie the knot. And it's why every move in the dating game has to be made with caution, patience and a praying **if you actually want to ply through that route of dating.**

There is a reason why the above sentence is made bold, we would find out much later as we read on.

An author and endometriosis warrior gave a very detailed and deep analysis of dating and courtship.

Dating is   Courtship is

Dating is	Courtship is
Eventful	Intentional
Gameplay	Build vision
Pleasureful	Purposeful
Ends with another date	Ends in marriage
No accountability	Accountability
Human decisions	Holy decisions

Personally, as a certified relationship therapist and marriage counselor, I have been so bothered about some dynamics in the dating phase; sometimes these dynamics come as questions during my counseling sessions as well.

Have you ever wondered why sex and all of its activities doesn't get projected in a friendly phase? Because that phase makes sex and it's activities look like it's the dating phase that can give you and your partner the freedom to explore and bond more, not knowing that you can still achieve the same results in a detailed friendship phase without exploring the options of erotic dimensions. But this is easier to do this when you both are on the same page.

This is why online dating platforms is fast becoming a channel where people are constantly heart broken, so what are the indices that your partner is supposed to be found online?

And how come it is easier to tell someone you have never seen before that you love him or her? This is because attraction of any realm can be physical or online and it doesn't matter how the attraction comes up, what should be considered is the reason why you are attracted to this person and if it is enough to consider doing life with him or her for life.

Another lie of the dating phase is that, longevity in togetherness is not equal to a successful marriage life. You can be wrongly paired with someone wrong for you for a long time and still end up being sad in your marriage. This why when some counselees reach out to me to state their issues, they will be like, "and we dated for long and I didn't see this part of him in all my years of being with him, and this is what will bring me to this deep question already, **why do we have several broken homes or broken marriages in spite of lengthy dating phases.** This will bring me to say that for a health of a togetherness to be tested and trusted in the confines of a marriage, it will be in the quality of moments shared before marriage and not the quantity of promises made to be together..

A counselee came up with this mind boggling question after so many years of rigmarolling and trying to find balance with different dating relationships and getting married.

And here are the answers she came up with, which she shared with me.

- **Could it be because it is phase that gets me closer to the person I want to marry?**
- **Could it be because all my friends are married or getting married?**
- **Could it be because I won't be friends with whom I'm dating and be able to date who was never my friend?**
- **Or could it be that whatever I can see in the friendship is possibly what I can still see in this person in the dating phase?**

I have also being very worried about the dimensions of short meet ups and drilled a friendship phase that gives you both an opportunity to study each other properly and when there is an opportunity to express how one feels (the man's perspective now), there is really nothing to be doing in the dating phase anymore, all he does is to ask the lady to just marry him already because there is really nothing to experiment in the dating phase especially when he is interested in keeping things pure.

We also have people who have known themselves for a long time and just jumped into preparing for their wedding just because they feel , they know each other already. And let me please emphasize that, spending a short time as friends or not even friends at all, before talking about marriage is not a guarantee that it won't work out successfully too.

On very special scenarios, especially when God is leading a person to marriage, it can be very precise, intentional, spontaneous and marriage may be some months after and they will go ahead and still have a great marriage, discovering a lot about themselves more in the confines of marriage and because, it is with God's leading, they are able to find balance.

But let me also warn, that God being involved in a marriage arrangement does not mean it will be automatically all rosy. It takes work to make it work too. So a marriage God orchestrated Himself will show problems TALKLESS of the one you designed yourself..

What is clear to note is that God is leading you into a detailed friendship phase that you want to build into marriage without necessarily not trying to explore what the dating dimension brings or you now trying to do dating because of the age and time we have found ourselves in but still staying close to the principles I shared earlier. But basically, it has to be based on the will of God to guide you on the particular routes to follow and methodology to use too

But also bear in mind that everything, God has designed has a counterfeit coordinated and given by the devil including the formula for meeting who you are supposed to with for life and this is where the infiltration has come in using the route of dating already.

Stay tuned….

There are different entities interested in destiny fulfillment. These entities are actually three. And they are:- God, because He created us in His image and already has a designed destiny for all His creatures (Jeremiah 1:5),then the Devil, because he has come to steal kill and to destroy (John 10:10) and then Man, i.e., we humans, i.e. "Us", because we are living a borrowed life, because it is an error to die not utilizing all we are meant to do (James 4:13-14).

The devil knows he has a short time to operate and so, what he does is to access likely ways of swaying God's creatures away from their destiny fulfillment. So what has he already done? He studied the ways of men and their activities and made most of what takes their time, efforts and involvements and he realized that human beings are often carried away with how to get married in life.

Building companionship has been our worry, from time immemorial, even in the bible, Adam needed a companion. Isaac needed a companion as well after his mom died and Abraham his father went out of his way to get a wife for him from amongst his people. Jacob also in a move to get a companion was enslaved, was deceived for 14years and he was even drugged and the wrong woman was given to him after the first seven years.

 Moses needed a companion and he started working for Jethro the priest and before long, Zipporah came into the picture. Samson also needed a companion, but he missed it terribly in his methodologies, and several others just to mention a few.

So even from the very first marriage in Genesis 3:1-5, the devil has always gotten involved in the affairs of man right from the very get go, without being invited. Remember the case of job too, when the devil engaged God in a conversation about inflicting Job's physical body with sickness and taking away everything he had, just to know if he will curse God or not?

His own wife, who is supposed companion, was even used as a potential tool of distraction, but thank God Job didn't succumb to the pressure. The bible tells us how we are unique in the sight of God created to fulfill divine mandate and it is quite evident how the devil does not really appreciate this esteemed point of view that God has about us.

It went on to say that we as humans are created a little lower than the angels and we are in a capacity and position to even judge these angels, but it might be an uphill task if one or two things go wrong in our quest to fulfill one of God's mandate here on earth which is to get it right it maritally. Bear in mind that, even though the bible expressly said that we should multiply and have dominion, it is also imperative to increase in numbers with the suitable methodology with the right person for you as well.

This is true. So with this position that we have found ourselves in by adoption and grace, all the devil needs to do is to bring up distractions that sways us away and reminds us more of our errors, problems and makes us forget our status as sons of God. By default, no creature of God is supposed to miss it maritally.

Look at it this way, God chose for Adam, and that would have been how it will look like for everyone too even if we have been given this permissive will to exercise and flex our muscles with choices we can muster within our armpits. A lack of relationship between man and God has even made it difficult for God to choose for us and even when He does, we sometimes even want to choose for ourselves, and then ask God for His choice. There is a reason why it is called God's will, more like He also has a point of view too.

We need to understand that for everything God has created, there is a counterfeit version.

There is a makeshift arrangement, an exact prototype designed to confuse us. For example, in 2 Corinthians 11:13-15, Exodus 7:10-12(magicians threw down their staffs and it became serpents just like Moses's staff). There is a developed system always that comes in that fashion and manner so that confusing people becomes very easy. God orchestrated miracles starting with a "M" and the devil came up with magic starting with "M" too. Even when Christ came to die for mankind, an antichrist has been mooted too.

The bible in Matthew 24:5 says, many will come in my name, claiming that "I am Christ and will deceive many. But what does that "in my name" means? It means that there will be a system of deception; a system of distraction is a system of confusing you if you are not strong in faith or if you are the kind of Christian drinking milk instead of eating bones.

How can we command power in the secret place when we still have pastors who are actively confusing Christians, filling them up with lies, with lies, sucking the breasts of ladies in order to cast out spirits and demons, forcing their members to drink antiseptic solutions all in the name of deliverance sessions and a lot of crazy things perpetrated in the church today. No wonder, the bible in 1st John 4 versus 1 says, Beloved, believe not every spirit, but test all spirits whether they are of God, because many false prophets are gone out in to the world.

So, I can authoritatively say that based on personal experience, personal encounters with married counselees and unmarried counselees and a deep revelation from God, that the dating phase is a satanically implanted phase by the devil, to make it look like the real deal.

It has gradually come to replace what God wanted and even created. The dating phase looks like what God intended in appearance but very toxic and damaging when you are in it. It has become the devil's most important tool for making believers miss it maritally, for unsuspecting young minds who do not know their left from their right to think that they are on the right track and it has led many astray and many soul tie covenants are being formed.

This confirms what the bible in Revelation chapter 12 versus 12 says, says 'Rejoice ye heavens and all who dwell in it, but woe to the earth and the sea, for the enemy is filled with fury and he had come down upon you for he knows he hath but a short time.

This explains why his sole aim is to decongest and depopulate the kingdom of heaven and then populate his kingdom. Marrying who God wants for you is a sure way of fulfilling your destiny and the devil knows that it is a very key area he can penetrate with his fury. You can see how Samson missed it maritally and ended the way he did.

What many people do not know is that, the devil secretly set up a school to derail so many people from understanding what God wants for them. We need to understand that anything God has created has a prototype and the school of dating is that prototype that the enemy orchestrated to resemble the particular school ordained for His children in order for them to get it right martially in life.

Unfortunately, a lot of people have enrolled in this school of dating unknowingly. Many have even lost their sense of belonging, many have even spent so much time in this school and by the time they realize what is going on, they become too old for the school God originally designed for them.

In my years of experience and study, I have come to realize that the devil uses our inexperience and lack of knowledge against us to keep us in perpetual darkness and makes us feel like there is something in particular that is wrong with us if we do not become students in this school of dating. I also realized that the negative program of the enemy to keep us impatient and yearning for who is not missing makes us want to be like other students in the school of dating so that we can have a feeling we are in tuned with how to get it right.

Also, I have come to realize the devil introduces the works of the flesh in our lives to speed up a desire to be a student in the school of dating. He even goes as far as making Christians to be oblivious of their God-given fruits through the ministry of the Holy Spirit in us, just like how it is written in Galatians 5:22-23.

Unfortunately, when the fruits of the Holy Spirit are not at work in our lives, we become susceptible to the available works of the flesh and this eventually catalyzes our missing it maritally.

When a person becomes born again, he or she becomes a carrier of the Holy Spirit that becomes resident as the comforter and friend according to (John 14:16). Therefore, the Holy Spirit automatically makes you to be a recipient of His fruits.

These are supposed to be feasible, and also portray the characteristics of a Christian, so we are supposed to be continually maturing towards Christ's likeness and in the word of God in order for us to understand how the Holy Spirit guides us into not making errors in our quest to be married.

As fate would have it, the devil has seen this, he is quite aware of the privileges we stand to gain, he is also aware of the fact that he needs to come in between us and the Holy Spirit to confuse us, give us frivolities, make us chase what or who is not missing and then shut down the Holy Spirit in our lives by making us grief the Holy Spirit on a daily basis confirming his secret agenda and activity in (Galatians 5:17), which says that for the flesh wrestles or lusteth against the spirit and the spirit against the flesh.

There is what we call "peril" of dating. And that peril means danger; it also means serious and immediate danger. We need to know that the dating phase has been tagged as the "let's get to know each other more" phase. The dating phase has now been tagged as the "how do we claim to know ourselves, if we don't date?" phase. The dating phase has become very experimental and elementary.

The dating phase has become the center of attraction for many young people that are bored. There is a system set up as a makeshift arrangement for what God originally designed and prepared. There is a system prepared for ignorant people to miss it maritally. This system has been set up for a very long time now, to the extent that even Google may not be able to even give accurate information if asked about its inception.

This system is very old deep, it is mystical. It is real. I mean, if you went through the introduction properly, you will understand why this system has come to stay. It is staged up as a distraction till Christ comes and a never ending mounted edifice that is negative to derail people. This system sadly has successfully played its way into the society, embraced by all and sundry, appreciated by both the young and the old, eagerly experimented by the ignorant and punishes those who break its rules.

This system has swallowed the mighty, the low, the poor, rich and even believers and unbelievers. This system, because of its long range foundation, its activities has to be seen as normal and thoroughly helpful. This system is seen as normal by Christians, preached by clergies and encouraged as well. The activities of this system are very confusing to man too, very innocent looking and it comes with a rage to be involved in.

This system has a shock absorber to wade off any other plot to truncate its activities. This system makes provision for availability, trust, speed and fake fulfillment. This system is so old to the point that no one bothers to check the authenticity of its source, outcome, existence, exposure and depth.

Since everything God created has a counterfeit, this system has made it possible for a counterfeit to occur on how many people get married in relationship life. This system has made the friendship phase to be an oversight and the courtship phase to be a lecture no longer needed by a student.

This system has made it possible that certain sweet words cannot be overlooked neither can they be forgotten. This system is designed and coordinated by one man with an an agenda to keep depopulating God's kingdom and populating his own. If Christian books, authors, Christian movies can't effectively detect this system, it then tells us of how deep and constructed it is.

This system is like a complete human system with different functions aimed at maintaining movement, forward progression, balance, growth and mobility. The circulatory part of this system makes sure that the evil plan is carried out to the latter and then men should also never have a reason not to date. (This explains why you are looked at as a fool when you talk about the non-existence of the dating phase).

This system lives with us, bathes with us, eats with us, grows with us and gets to introduce itself to our children and grow with them too, we call it exposure and experience and knowledge, not knowing that this system just gets revitalized and renewed. This system is just like a pregnant woman and how she gets to grow bigger and bigger until she puts to bed. The birth of that baby and the ability for that baby to grow and take on that incentive can be likened to this system. What then is his system? **"The system of the dating phase"**.

A phase where people believe everything is allowed, it's a phase of experimentation. It's a phase where people need to get it right. It's a phase where people think they need to explore. It's a phase where people believe you are supposed to get to know each other. It's a phase of flaw detection and character measurement.

It's a phase of behavior analysis "I need to be careful mentality". A phase of if it does not work out, everyone can then go their separate ways. A phase of "I won't even beg her, if he or she doesn't listen to my pleas, then she should just forget it. A phase of, "I will change but let me enjoy some things a bit and I will change but let me not just display my character for now, after all we are not married yet" a phase of "if you love me, you will understand". Actually, the dating phase is a counterfeit from the enemy himself. The dating phase is a direct opposite of what God wanted and planned.

The dating phase when in place is the only way, the devil can stay in shape and get his plan ongoing about depopulating God's kingdom and populating his own. The dating phase is a phase where people are doing things on their own. So here is a question I always ask people. It's one of the most important questions in relationship life.

So here it goes; **"If you remove I LOVE YOU from a dating phase and you intend to keep it pure and holy, what can you not achieve in the friendship phase?"** Nobody has been able to tell me otherwise. So, the devil has kept many people wishing for more and many are tired of the emotional power of those words in capital.

Even in my counseling sessions, whenever I ask this particular question, they end up telling me, there is nothing in particular to be achieved if friendship is to be maintained and results gotten.

God's real prescription that has been hidden away from many people is in this order: - FRIENDSHIP---- COURTSHIP---MARRIAGE. He doesn't want a phase where you need to try and study someone one in particular specially and this is why you have a phase for expression in the friendship. The dating phase is a way of choosing for yourself and doing it. This is what has led to abortion, kissing, heavy hugs and pettings, sex and undefined togetherness.

Dating is a way of us saying we choose for ourselves. Dating is a way of telling ourselves that we can on our own detect who people are truly are in that phase, people we didn't create.

The dating phase makes you to be oblivious and unconcerned and less observant of what the friendship phase can be. The dating phase almost pushes you away from the friendship phase before you are able to discover some red flags, this explains why red flags are not spotted or taken seriously because the dating system bathes you with the emotions to weaken your decision making when danger is even in sight. The dating phase convinces you that you are doing quite well and all you need is already given especially because you are seeing and hearing lots of emotions from this other person you are in that togetherness with.

There is a rage against every teenager and unmarried young person to make them see the foolishness in enjoying the friendship and going into a system called dating as if there is actually something to be discovered there.

The dating system is like the amusement park you want to really go to and on getting there, you find out that your favorite ride is faulty.

God is saying if someone is bad, you can easily figure out in the friendship phase, but the devil is saying you can figure out in the dating phase too, which is usually not the truth because you will be blinded by lots of distractions and filled with emotional sentiments that will hamper your mettle in taking tough decisions such as exiting that complicated relationship already. Because of this, many people have married and regretted their decisions every day.

This can be likened to the two trees in the garden of Eden i.e. God is saying you may eat of the tree of life and any other but the devil is saying eat of the tree of good and evil. But this is only a ploy to make you bond souls sexually, then get your organs violated and then make it difficult to observe or spot red flags and also make a concise decision about leaving.

God didn't design the dating phase. This system was orchestrated as a counterfeit to give people a feeling of false love and false peace since they are generally important and need attention. God doesn't want a long togetherness that will lead to errors. He is not against friendships and He feels that if everyone is friends with each other and have their companies defined, they will easily tell who is ripe for marriage through their personal evaluation and deep conviction in the spirit.

This is why people date for 5, 6, and 7 years and still have issues in marriage. I mean, why? Why is it that a long dating phase is not equal to a good marriage? Because a good marriage is not even what God is after, He is after a kind of marriage named after Him called GODLY.

Why the break up after a long dating? Because you intentionally prolonged what you saw in the beginning or observed or didn't want to admit or just because you feel everyone needs time. If you are married, how far now? What's your story? If you are in the dating phase, who is leading you? What did you achieve in the friendship phase? And if you are single, what is it that you are looking at going forward?

Are you looking out for a dating phase? A longer process that you feel will guarantee you the time to know your partner better. Or are you looking for a friendship phase that can edify you and bring out the best out of you? Or are you looking at practicing certain steps in dating phase just like a lot of people are doing out there in order to explore and satisfy their curiosity?

CHAPTER FOUR: MY PERSONAL EXPERIENCES AND COUNSELLING SESSIONS

In my years of understanding the mysteries of personal finding, and counseling counselees (both married and unmarried), I have realized over time that one of the errors made from most married people is that they do not understand how confusing and tricky the dating system is really about and all they do is to go ahead to jump at it, thereby exposing themselves to many problems that can be avoided. Sadly, they jump into it with so much excitement and expectation just because of the rave of the moment.

On a personal note, it took me many years of repeated mistakes, of falling and rising, before I could come up with this mystery with the help of the Holy Spirit. One day, while I was having a deep meditation in my spirit, I began to have a heavy impression in my heart about the dating system and gradually, I started having a mental picture about the whole thing, like it was so real in my heart and I realized that as soon as a question came up in my head, I would almost immediately get an answer for it. It looked like a deep mystery discovered, it looked confusing and baseless to a whole lot of people, yet it is the actual truth.

Sometimes when counselees reach out to me on my private whatsapp counseling bay platform and tell me about a failing marriage or failed relationship, it is easy to trace this situation to the fact that little or nothing was done to checkmate the ignorance level. This will be the case because; you can't give what you don't have. Sadly, many people don't have this information.

In fact, it will interest you that are reading this book to know, that many Christian books and journals and many preachers talk about dating as a major step towards finding or being found right.

I'm not saying this is not a phase that has not proven successful for some people, but it actually depends on what you call success, because I have found out in my counseling experiences that so many couples living together are not friends of themselves at all, there wasn't any confluence point to meet up and that is why it is as if things get boring between couples in the confines of marriage because a major phase was skipped and they were busy being too emotionally inclined in the dating phase before they got married.

This is why the rage of the enemy against mankind on the subject of DATING can't be overemphasized

Sometimes, when I ask married women how long they were friends with their husbands before they got married to them, they will tell me 3 weeks or 2 months and you hear them spending several years dating each other? Doing what exactly? When it will be like one is married to a total stranger. So, does this mean one can't be friends with someone, date either short or long and even go ahead to court and get it right martially? The answer is No.

Yes you can, but you will be doing a lot of things on your own, operating with your permissive will, relying on luck to not disappoint or partner, or not get disappointed just because you have seen the success stories of people you know in your shoes already.

Personally, I have come to realize the speed at which people use to cross over into this delicate and deadly and dangerous satanically implanted phase. Mathematically, it is safe to know now that the devil is basically an enemy of the friendship phase, because he feels the longer you wait or dwell in that phase, the easier it is for you to get a clarity on how to take the best decision and move on and start finding yourself, which he doesn't want.

Many people have lost their virginities before realizing the danger of dating; many people have dwelled in long relationships playing HUSBAND and WIFE roles to the wrong people before realizing their foolishness. Many people have spent years looking for what is not missing and allowed their emotions to rule them ahead of very detailed information they are supposed to have access too.

Early in my formative years too, my status as an only child didn't make me learn things properly from a mystical point of view. I always knew that getting immoral is bad, but I never really understood that been in a time wasting togetherness especially one that could be capable of exposing you to immorality could weaken your emotions and not make one to take the best decision.

If 50% of the world's population today who are mature enough for marriage can understand the scheme of the enemy concerning the dating system and make the conscious efforts to enjoy the friendship phase and not get trapped by the lies of the dating phase and live their lives with a mentality that marriage itself is not an achievement, then there will be a massive crediting of the accounts in heaven and lots of boxes will be ticked and heaven will get more populated and hell will get more depopulated.

If this mystery is discovered by more individuals, then many sexual activities that have succeeded in keeping people in redundant position will stop. We are where we are today because of the influences, peer group pressures from a society that sees an average teenager or growing youth as a small boy or girl with no common sense if he or she refuses to be in a dating relationship, social media vices, songs, groups in school, even churches make it very available and possible for this dating phase to be taken on as an incentive and practiced.

Today, unwanted pregnancies, ruptured tummies through abortions sessions and covenants spiritually through physical sex are now the order of the day. So many people really do think it is just normal to be in a dating phase, this can even be one of the weirdest things to hear when you do not know what this is about.

Most of my counselees have jumped from one relationship to another just to find solace in affection, love and checkmate connection. Some of them just believe that the best way to get found right or to find right is to just keep searching for dating flings and that if you do not try it out, how do you know the good person for you out there?

 One will think life is just so perfect already with someone who appears just perfect when someone who is in a dating phase but you may be blind to see the true picture because the dating phase most times is an intentional revealer except , unless God decides to show you mercy.

I remember how many years ago, I would want to start up relationships with women without even being friends with them and by the time we had gone halfway the line and I notice a behavior very annoying, I would be like, what's this? How did we get here? Or why am i just knowing this? But the funny question should is, "which other platform have I provided or laid as a foundation to show me this person's true character?

Because of my status as a loner, my late mom was very passionate about me getting married before she died. She really wanted to be a part of all my successful stories. She knew she wouldn't be around for too long and desperately wanted to see me get married.

My mother was someone I couldn't say a "no" to at all in anything she wanted. I remember how she made me meet many young ladies, of course with the permission and cooperation of their parents to try and see if we could be an "item", thankfully none of those dimensions worked out, it was usually because, the ladies didn't connect with me, or because they didn't like the fact that their parents were suggesting who they should marry to them or I also didn't connect with them too.

This is why you should not joke with two young people who grew up as childhood friends, who decide to be together for the rest of their lives. You would be surprised as to how they can have a perfect understanding of each other even without bringing God into the equation. (Although, the GOD FACTOR is always important, but it is not the only reason why you will enjoy your marriage.) There is always a place of physical work.

Going forward, through my experiences with women I had relationships with back then, i realized the ideal model of a "normal" togetherness of two young people who want to make God center of their lives and decisions revolved around questions like:-

- How was your night?
- What are your visions?
- What are your ten year plans?
- What have you eaten today?
- What was your last memory verse?
- When was the last time you heard from dad and mom?
- Am I seeing you in church this evening?
- What's your idea about having so many kids?
- Who are your mentors?

And many other questions related to all of these. But here is where I'm heading to, if these kind of questions pop up in Godly relationship, what makes it any different if they are asked in a friendship relationship?

I also realized that whilst questions like these are asked, you are having a daily understanding of the kind of person he or she is and if you are both compatible behaviorally, you are growing together and sharing visions, rubbing minds, bonding and synergizing in harmless manner with no pressures on trying to prove you love this person in the confusing confines of a dating phase.

Imagine having this kind of friendship for as long as five to seven years and you are seriously now considering who to settle down with. Your efforts in finding, who you want to spend the rest of your life with, will actually be easier. Why? Because you have someone who you have an existing bond with, especially if they are very single just as you are.

You will agree with me that this is not what the devil wants because he knows this makes God's creatures to be more profound in doing better when it comes to either settling down or when properly married already. You will also need to bear in mind that you can deeply and truly have deep feelings for yourselves and keep it expressed with relevant and sensitive questions that will give an idea to the other person and make them see you as an option they need to actually consider, while you secretly wish and pray that God orders your steps and the other person when it's time to settle down.

But imagine when you meet each other online and start dating out rightly, or you even met physically and exited the friendship phase just after three weeks just because you both want to secure a space in your lives without proper understanding, you will agree with me that your depth together can't be as rich as the people in an intentional friendship phase I talked about earlier.

Now, let us look at a list of statements for people who in a dating relationship, either they met online on some social media or even physically. **Bear in mind that you must always defend your words in the dating phase and this is where so many people are left vulnerable already.**
Here are some questions that I now would resonate with you:-
- I miss you so much (you have to prove you miss him or her somehow, because when you don't, it means you are not saying the truth.
- I love you so much. (You also have to prove you actually mean what you have said, because when you don't, it means you don't mean what you have said.

- When are we seeing each other? (Seeing each other comes with responsibilities. This is where grounds are shifted, boundaries are invaded, privacy broken down, people passing the night in each other's houses and sex going down or sex related activities as well.)

These three statements are just top on the list. You will notice that as friends you ask more questions on what you need to know to take a decision but quite funny enough these questions may never come up in a dating phase because of the distractions it comes with, and even if they come up, they may not come with the best results one would have expected to see either in a friendship phase or courtship phase.

Infact there was a time I started throwing it to my female counselees that want to be in relationships. Asking them to ask guys who talk to them about dating after few weeks of being friends or having skipped the friendship phase totally, what they (the guys) feel they want to achieve in the dating phase that they feel they can't achieve in the friendship phase?

This move has ended up confusing these guys. Most times, they don't even know what to answer and they either get angry at these female counselees of mine or look for something out of the blue that may not even make sense to tell them. This tells you how deep this system is and must be ventured into with wisdom and understanding.

These days, only hunger and consistency will make one to see the dangers of dating, know them and decide not just to go celibate, but also make a conscious decision to be comfortable in the friendship phase or the ALONE phase. Looking at it very keenly from a liberal point of view, it may be so impossible or stupid, but if one accesses things from a deeper angle with an eye of understanding, one will realize that, this can even get to be one of the deepest discussions in relationship life just yet if you look at how dating itself crept into our world and how purity has been rubbished.

CHAPTER FIVE: THE EIGHT LOVE LANGUAGES AND THE DATING PHASE

The popular Gary Chapman came up with 5 love languages in one of his books that helped in stabilizing many relationships and marriages. But in recent times, based on my personal counseling experiences with counselees, I came to realize that these love languages could actually run to eight because of the depth of relationship life itself.

The community of relationship life is so broad with key sections that are worthy of knowledge, which are still going to be looked at keenly in this chapter like: the 7 schools of relationship life, and 31 reasons why you should not even marry someone and the 9 ingredients of relationship life.

So, here are the eight love languages and we are going to see how marrying them with the dating phase makes the dating phase all the more dangerous and dicey to initiate.

Here:-

- Love language of service
- Love language of quality time
- Love language of giving gifts
- Love language of encouragement
- Love language of affirmation
- Love language of respect
- Love language of patience
- Love language of physical touch (only in marriage, but now breached).

The funny thing is that the devil does not care if you can speak any of these languages; his only worry is that he does not want us speaking them to people who will easily understand.

It is possible to speak a certain love language to your partner with clear intentions and that relationship still may not be what God wants for you. For example, if you start living with someone, you are not married to and you both speak the love language of service to each other, under the platform of a dating relationship, things may look rosy for that moment, but then you are fast forwarding what you should be really doing with another person and this might leave room for plenty of pretense

It is even possible that you both might not have sex but there can be a shifting of grounds like kissing and heavy petting and the rest. Now if the lady for example, likes the way you speak the love language of service to her and probably she didn't have someone in her past relationships who did or didn't see her parents speaking that particular love language, she may automatically conclude that she has met the right person and she will do all she can to keep the relationship, this will lead to her having a kind of false peace in the relationship.

We must be mindful of the love languages we allow into our lives especially when we do not have what it takes to be married; it is possible to successfully access a particular love language from a wrong person who just decides to speak the particular language just to lure you into a relationship and eventually sex, or who is just skilled in a negative way.

Just imagine someone who has learnt how to give or speak the love language of quality time out in previous relationships and you for example as a woman who craves for it badly because she didn't deal with her loneliness, funny enough, they can't be discovered in the dating relationship phase, because the dating phase doesn't present itself as a platform to discover such details.

All of a sudden, after the wedding you will discover that the reason why you felt he is your husband was because he spoke perfectly to you the love language of quality time and you will really need more, because that's all he is probably going to offer you. So what now? Quality time for sex, communication that won't yield the results geared towards success in marriage.

Sincerely, we need to be very careful about the platform we are going into relationships, there is a reason why I say there 31 reasons not enough to get married to someone, but these same reasons are why people consider who they have in their lives for marriage sometimes or most times even, the speed of reasons at which people initiate relationships are because they are overly swept off their feet on how so expertly the person they like effortlessly speaks a certain love language they appreciate to them.

Sometimes, a lady can be so heartbroken because of an issue or the other and comes in contact with a man who naturally speaks the love language of encouragement and does it so effortlessly, now if boundaries are not set up and carelessness is involved, an unplanned relationship can begin that makes the guy to be a messiah in her life, obviously the reason for the connection is purely based on emotions that grew because of the love language spoken or heard and not because any effort was made to school each other in a detailed friendship phase.

Love languages are behavioral in nature. They can be worked on, they can be improved, one can even be so holy, Godly and righteous and lack a certain love language that the partner really needs to hear regularly.

 So getting a partner who speaks a certain love language so effortlessly to you in a dating phase is not a guarantee that you are functioning under the calendar of God's will for you, there may be so many underlying factors you didn't take into considerations that can haunt you much later.

What can be very obtainable is when you both start off under the umbrella of a platonic relationship platform and school each other and then shoot shots of the respective love languages under your belt that you can muster at every opportunity that you get, of course, there is still a realm you both may not be able to access in that friendship phase but this is where you need God's guidance because if He is involved, He will make everything so easy between the both of you as time goes on and as intentions are made known but it won't be under a system of test running each other like what the dating system of nowadays relationships brings.

Sincerely speaking, many people have asked me this question am about to ask now. Coach; you always speak of the lies of this dating phase always, but supposing after doing a good job at the friendship phase and then you pop the big question and you are doing your courtship, what is the progress you are bound to make?

And I tell you people this, you really can't know the real and entire make up of who you are getting married to all at once at the spur of the moment, and I tell people that, you not telling this person you love him or her and not highlighting the basis of togetherness as a dating affair has put you in a position where you are not one of those persons who is saying "we can just take a walk if it doesn't work out".

So taking the big step of asking someone to marry you after your efforts in a detailed friendship phase as a man to establish familiarity means it's a step you are taking with the permission of God, as if to say that you are not doing this on your own and you are down with the person no matter what; that you are not going to back out because God is leading you, so this is what most dating relationships miss out on, key questions like genotypic compatibility , tribal issues are not talked about, we are not even talking about what the will of God is all about now.

But you can have a friendship that is 100% maintained if you know the answers to some key questions by default and then take it to prayers and if you still get a NO from God, you would not even need to pop any question at all because you will sense it in your spirit that not all friendships should go to the next phase, but sadly how many people have the profile to be patient, seeking God's will? When 75% of the people out there are already frustrated that they are not into one relationship or the other.

The truth is marriage does not change people. But it can improve you if you are hungry enough for a change. Many people consciously or unconsciously married people who are not speaking the love language that naturally brings the best out of them. It is very possible for God to orchestrate a certain relationship for you geared towards marriage, with all the clarity and convictions, one will still have issues in his her marriage. Is that shocking?

No! It shouldn't, this means God doesn't create a perfect marriage but He can create a marriage with two hungry people ready to work towards perfection, working on their flaws and weaknesses and also learning to speak the love languages that can better the mood and provide comfort for the both of them.

The right formula is a very straight forward affair, yet so complicated if not followed. The right formula can become injurious to a person if boycotted and deviated from. The right formula can become difficult to do and adhere to, if it is not done at the right time and with the right person. For everything, in life, there is a set pattern, there is a code of conduct, there is a system of getting it done in a particular format, once this pattern is breached, and then there will be a lot of factors that will go wrong in one's relationship life.

The bible is clear on this one, in psalm 11:3, which says, if the foundation be destroyed, what can the righteous do? There are only two things to do and they are; identification of the destroyed foundation and addressing the root cause of the destroyed foundation, and sometimes prayers are not enough, it may come with ardent steps towards making difficult decisions. It comes with plenty pains and sacrifices, and efforts and payment of prices, just like what the bible says in James 2:26; for faith without works is dead.

The right formula is first of all, friendship, secondly, courtship and then the marriage phase. But if you both must go through the dating phase, it has to be in accordance with the word of God based on the principles I mentioned earlier in the book. But the structure that makes it quite comfortable to serve Him whole heartedly without confusion is this three laid down phases already.

We can deceive ourselves to think that there is a friendship phase dimension which cannot be as authentic or effective as the dating phase, but permit me to say this, there is a cryptic phase that comes up only when an intention is known which can be seen as a phase that will allow the buttressing of flaws and weaknesses but with marriage in view, we can't deceive ourselves anymore as to how two people who are just friends, but one would just imagine things in his or her head that an undefined courtship filled with sex and it's activities is the next thing on the card.

When someone who is God's will for you, speaks a certain love language to you, even as early as the friendship phase, it is easier for you to build on that information in the place of prayer. God Himself won't bring someone that is 100% perfect; He brings someone you have to take time to understand in the school of patience, so this means that patience can be a school and also a love language.

A certain love language can be spoken so perfectly by a wrong person in a dating phase, and if this is the reason why marriage would be considered by him or her then, missing it martially may not be inevitable.

This is why you must be careful in your getting happy that someone is effortlessly speaking a certain love language you crave for so much or because you didn't grow up to see your parents speaking it amongst themselves, you just forget about compatibility, connectivity and conformity and just automatically give in to what you call love in your mind of decisions.

This is the reason why I always emphasize that being good is not enough, and that being Godly is not also enough, and so what is enough is God's own will. One can be a believer and naturally didn't grow up with a certain love language that may be too necessary to be spoken to you.

We need to understand that God is the ULTIMATE MATCH MAKER who created everyone in His image and likeness and knows our make-up, flaws and weaknesses (because He intentionally didn't create anyone perfect, but we can grow better and work towards perfection).

But this is a fact the devil doesn't want people to remember. Why many people are having issues in their marriages today is because they don't understand that, **it is difficult to make God to be Omega over what He was never Alpha over. There are processes and prices must be paid somehow.**

Speaking of love languages will come naturally by the exploration of the NATURE AND NURTURE dynamics in a person's life and the fluency, speed and consistency will be based on what was mustered growing up. Being good can guarantee some platform to speak it to your partner but we would be brought on our knees at some point, as if to say that we need God's touch in our lives to speak effectively.

Many homes are under fire today because of not much is even known about the persons they married. Many people are married to total and complete strangers. Imagine a female counselee aged 36 years, just waking up one morning and parking her things back to her father's house?
What could have led to this? It is only when the job was not properly done in the friendship phase.

Today, we see many people who are not really Godly and who are not carrying spiritual things on their hands having a bit of stability in their marriages because they were friends together for years before making an intention and decision to marry each other.

The problem with such togetherness is that over familiarity can make sex so easily accessible which is not supposed to be experienced at all in any of the phases in relationship life except in marriage.

When you look at questions like, can I find a man who will be sexually compatible with me and understand my emotional needs if i decide not to explore in the dating phase and trust God for His will? Yes! Because God Himself is the Almighty match maker and if only we can have an idea of what our potential partners are capable of with better understanding, many people would probably wait to trust God for His will.

But, no one is smarter than God. When God sees you taking steps of exploration in a dating phase He didn't sanction, then He gets the signal that you are omitting Him from the equation and the set standard He has laid down and your actions in the whole package becomes like an accident waiting to happen.
It will take discernment to know what God is saying about a certain relationship, but you can simply have Him to order your steps if you stay closer to His leadings and there is no way He will put you up with someone who will lead you astray.

There is a word I have been using in this book over time. This word has led many astray. This word has made people to miss it martially. This word has made many to have a wrong mentality and mindset on the kind of steps they are supposed to be taking. This word has made many to shift grounds, satisfied the creature more than the creator, and it has made many to look for what is not missing.

This word is called love. It is not possible to write a book like this and not talk about love. There is a mystery about love. We only know what you know. There are different types of love and there is a school called the school of love. Many have gotten enrolled in this school and still dropped out.

THE SCHOOL OF LOVE

The course of the person of love(God)
The course of love languages
The course of likeness
The course of "love as a process"
The course of counterfeit design (lust)
The course of "when love is not enough"
The course of "the mysteries of practiced love amongst mere mortals

I'm going to critically analyze the difference in all of these types of courses to be studied in the school of love. It is because many do not have the understanding that has made them miss it in life and just conclude that anything that comes close to having something for someone is to be interpreted as love and it is this factor that has made the devil use this school of ignorance to punish many people into jumping into wrong relationships, going into wrong marriages, carrying unwanted pregnancies, trying out what they should not be coming close to and finally looking for what is not missing. We just have to be guided.

- ## THE COURSE OF THE PERSON OF LOVE:-

1 John 4:8 describes one of God's primary attributes as love. This verse describes God's love as permeating His essence in all He is and all He does. Who is this "person of love"? He is God Himself. And love is His nature. We are, humans created in His image and likeness. This means that by default, we are supposed to carry over this nature of love, showing kindness and doing good to everyone around us, people should look at us and do not need to read the bible before seeing the manifestation of God's character in our lives, this make sense when you look at the bible in 2 Corinthians 5:20, Now then, we are ambassadors for Christ, as though God were pleading through us.

In demonstrating this kind of love called the AGAPE love, we must be regenerated, we must be born again, we must be blood washed, only then can we display this kind of love unconditionally to men, women, and children and even to our enemies.

- ## THE COURSE OF THE MYSTERIES OF THE PRACTICED LOVE AMONGST MERE MORTALS:-

Under this case, we are able to see two kinds of categories….

The first category (God Monitored category):- are about people who God have a blueprint for, they are like Samuel in the bible, which God was intentional about. It's like a "come rain, "come sun" scenario. He has already designed how the journey of their lives will pan out. They may physically try their best to get into diverse relationships and even get married too, but it won't work out for them because God will be at the back ground sponsoring their delay, if they try to live their lives as if they created themselves.

Two people can be apart in separate continents but He can bring them together at a set time to be married , it will be in a way that, if God has vested interests in these two persons, any relationship they go into on their own will not work out and He will personally see to their coming to fulfill destiny.

The second category (self-will category); -

 God stays out of the picture. But still has an in-depth idea of what is happening in their lives. He allows people in this category to utilize their willpower to choose in making their marital decisions.

He allows mortals to utilize and exercise their initiatives and intuitions and intellect coupled with their emotions to draw a conclusion for themselves. We have seen marriages under this category thriving. Where you don't see God communicating with them or interfering in their decisions, He only comes into the picture to bless their union.

What we can tell is that a strong force, that these persons interested in each other merges them together, can majority of this kind of marriage be God's will? Yes of course!

The only thing is that God gives them more room than the first category to express their will power... this is where utilizing of their permissive will becomes obvious, then they get blessings from God Himself. Most times, they usually get the job done based on the prayers of their late parents, mentors, destiny intercessors and the rest of them. So they don't even do much of the work because someone or some people had paid some prices in the confines of prayer altars.

THE COURSE OF LOVE LANGUAGES:

Gary chapman came up with five love languages that have been useful in this dispensation for many years now. But in my counseling ministry and experiences, I have come to realize that they are more than five in number.

- Love language of affirmation
- Love language of appreciation
- Love language of encouragement
- Love language of quality time
- Love of physical touch (only recommended in marriage)
- Love language of receiving gifts
- Love language of service
- Love language of respect
- Love language of patience

It is possible for a particular marriage to tick all the boxes of these love languages. It is possible to get it all right. There is no perfect marriage but there are excellent ones.

You can get stability and balance by growing up in realms and dimensions as you learn these languages because just like how you travel to a region with a particular language to be learnt before you can settle in to flow with the people there predominantly, you can still get to learn these languages so expertly and improve your relationship life and marriage.

Studying and passing this course it is what will guarantee your stability in relationship life and marriage.

THE COURSE OF "LOVE AS A PROCESS;-

This is where you need to know that love builds, love intensifies, and love is just like a muscle that grows bigger where it is flexed, stressed, exercised and worked on. It is in this course that you will be told that love can be killed and it can be kindled. It is in this course that you will be told that love is not enough and that it is not automatic. So there is a part of this mystery of love that comes with time, efforts, attitude and character to tarry in the" dissipating of energy phase" room of emotions waiting for your inputs to grow and pay off those really worked out muscles ready to be displayed.

THE COURSE OF "WHEN LOVE IS NOT ENOUGH":-

It is in this course you will get to know that there are nine ingredient that are key in the soup of relationship life and marriage that can dictate the taste of long lasting and effective bonding and synergy and love is not even one of them, love just comes as an added advantage, in this course, love is seen as a catalyst that can make a relationship reaction kick off better. Like I often say, love is not enough and love is not a hole people fall into, it is a path itself people walk in and through. I always often tell my counselees too that they don't fall in love, they rather walk in it, but when you fall in it, you will stand up with confusion and with bruises on the skin of your relationship life and marriage.

It is in this course that you will know that marrying only based on love is disastrous and you might want to ask a 50 year old woman if it's been just love that has been keeping her in a 20 year old union with her husband. Often times I have said it that there are nine ingredients of relationship life and long lasting marriage and love is not of them, because love itself is not even enough.

They are:- commitment, communication, compatibility, consistency, respect, trust, patience, transparency, and understanding.

The same way there are seven types of love and many are using EROS love as a yardstick or template to get married, forgetting that all the physical characteristics of a person can fade away but only the character will keep you in a marriage for a long time.

Many men have gotten married to women with big and pointed breast, so what happens when these breasts go down? What happens when the hips go out of shape? What happens when the buttocks gets out of shape? I am not saying you as a man should not get attracted to a man physically, but as soon as it becomes the bedrock of your decision making in a sensitive issue like settling down, then your marriage can be like an accident waiting to happen.

The foundation of a marriage is very important and once there is an error, it will affect the very totality of that marriage. There are 31 reasons why you can't just marry anybody and what is most important is God's will, but sadly, how many people have the profile to access this will of God for their lives? Quite funny enough, they are all reasons that are used as indices and could be seen as what is enough. But in my years of experiences counseling married women and men, they have used all of them to judge their reason why they eventually married someone in particular and they all failed at a point in time, so this is why the **GOD FACTOR** can't be trivialized. I'm going to be mentioning these 31 reasons shortly and I have also written a book on it as well by the grace of God titled **31 REASONS WHY YOU SHOULD NOT MARRY SOMEONE.**

<u>THE COURSE OF LIKENESS:-</u>

It is imperative to note that, there is no such thing as LOVE AT FIRST SIGHT but there is what we call, LIKENESS AT FIRST SIGHT. You can set your eyes on someone for the very first time and you will like something about them, could be about how they talk, walk or carry themselves, it could even be about a physical body feature, but then this likeness can serve as a platform if anything is to come up.

It is important that you are attracted to who you say you love and want to marry. If love is not enough, then likeness cannot be enough either. Love grows and it can be a process, it is just sheer ignorance and foolishness to say you just saw someone and fell in love with him or her, because love is not a hole you fall into.

When you meet someone you like, it is not even enough to say or conclude that he or she is the will of God for you, the person might be good but not good for you, the person might be a Godly Christian but not wired for you. When you say you love someone, it means you have scrutinized your heart and checkmated yourself by studying the seven types of love in the school of love to decipher what is propelling your move.

Since likeness is naturally embedded, it is wrongly used. One of the weirdest ways of answering a certain question I want to ask now is:-

Question: - Why do you love him or her??

Answer: - because I like him so much...

It is important to know that, you can't love who you don't like, but you can like who you don't love...This is why we are having marriages were people were never attracted to each other. I have had people reaching out to me telling me they don't seem to have any attraction whatsoever to the people they have married and living with already.

31 REASONS NOT ENOUGH TO MARRY SOMEONE

This section is so deep; actually, its details and depth can't be fully expounded here, as one will need to read a book on it properly. But just so you know that there are 31 reasons why you just can't marry someone you know or have come to like.

They are:-

- Love
- Likeness
- Pity
- Childhood friends
- From the same community
- Having the same goal and visions like you do
- Being good
- Being Godly
- Sponsored your education
- Escaping fornication
- For a child to have a father figure

- Same church member
- Referred from a mentor
- A successful friendship phase
- Genotypic compatibility
- Money
- Your friend's choice
- Wedding in the dream with him or her
- Effortlessly speaks your love languages
- Physical appearance
- Good manners
- First love
- Intelligence
- Parent's choice
- Understands people
- Financial helper
- Vastly exposed
- Being outspoken
- Opportunity to be sponsored in school
- Because the person didn't project sex before marriage
- Pregnant with a child already
- Because everyone else is getting married
- Peace of mind.

So what is enough then??
The answer is clear and straight forward:- God's will….But it is imperative to note that, accessing the will of God without having a relationship with Him will only be a fraudulent dream that one must wake up from already….

This book "THE LIES OF THE DATING PHASE" was birthed out of a deep and burning desire based on how things have gone from bad to worse in relationship life and marriage. People are now looking for what and who is not missing and the devil has used ignorance has a major tool to truncate the supposed stability we are supposed to have access to, in our dispensation today.

In my counseling sessions, I realized that there is a major arsenal the devil uses in this our dispensation to frustrate the efforts of many youths in relationship life, to make them to take wrong steps in choosing right, to make them explore realms they are not supposed to even come to. In my findings, I found out that the weapon of ignorance has been deployed for many years to achieve this purpose, marrying it with what the bible says about people being destroyed for lack of knowledge according to Hosea chapter 4 verses 6.

This book is an EYE OPENER into this satanic ploy the enemy has laid down, and still laying down and will still lay down aimed at depopulating the kingdom of God and populating the kingdom of the devil till the end of the age comes. This book also aims at giving people a full idea of what personal finding is all about especially when it comes to getting right in marriage.

Because sadly, frivolities are chased already….

Stephen Adegboye is a certified marriage counselor, relationship therapist, life coach, psychologist and also serves as a pastor in the mountain of fire and miracles ministries youth church region 5 in the city of Port Harcourt, Nigeria.

He has a BSC in General microbiology from the prestigious Madonna University also majored in medical microbiology in University of Port Harcourt all in rivers state.

He is the author of 31 REASONS WHY YOU SHOULD NOT MARRY SOMEONE and MY ADDICTION STORY which are on platforms like amazon, okadabooks and selar.

His relationship and marriage ministry name is called RELATIONSHIP LIFE WITH KUNLE and can be accessed on instagram, clubhouse, Facebook, MIXLR, twitter, tiktok, Google podcasts and YouTube.

By God's grace, he has so many audio messages on spotify, google podcasts, apple podcasts, amazon music, anchor and other listening platforms.